first time for everything

Editor: Tom Whitfield
Cover design and interior layout:
Angela K. Durden © 2018
www.angeladurden.com
www.sbp-music.com/spb-music

978-0-9854623-1-4
First Time for Everything
Publisher: Writer for Hire!
Imprint: Second Bight

9 780985 462314 >

This book is dedicated to all who inspire another.

"Ods life! must one swear to the truth of a song?"
Matthew Prior, "A Better Answer" (1718)

"What is the voice of song, when the world lacks the ear of taste?"
Nathaniel Hawthorne, "Canterbury Pilgrims" — The Snow Image (1851)

"Artists — by definition innocent — don't steal.
But they do borrow without giving back."
Ned Rorem, "Anatomy of Two Songs" — Music From Inside Out (1967)

On the advice of a friend, I bought Kenny Chesney's album, *Hemingway's Whiskey*. On it was a beautiful song, told from a man's point of view, written by three men, Lee Brice, Billy Montana, and Jon Stone. The song was called "Seven Days."

I fell in love with it. Rarely had I ever heard a song from a man's perspective that was so deep, and introspective. Telling of longing for reasons that had nothing to do with sex as the animal act, but sex as making love, as communication, as emotional need. The feeding of souls, the speaking truth to another when the mouth could not utter a sound.

The song was sad. I wondered why, in this case, there was no happily ever after. Then I asked myself, "Why can't the woman stay? What brought her there? Why did she leave? Did she ever think of the man again?"

To answer, I wrote "First Time for Everything". A song on this same scene, from the woman's point of view.

I have been accused of writing my songs and novels as if they were thinly veiled autobiography. I can say to you, here and now, that I only wish that were the case. I can definitively state I have never committed murder.

But from where do I get my ideas? How is it I can so accurately write about, oh...say...murder? That is what I do. I am a writer, after all.

Add to that, I am a sociopathic empath with an extremely high DNA vibration. This is a bad combination, keeping many people, including myself, confused.

How can a person attract and repulse multitudes of people, feel deeply and clearly and thoroughly and compassionately, be moved to help others out of their pain, but still not really care about anything or anyone?

It's a terrible way to live, but a great thing for a writer to be.

In other words, drama finds me, and all I have to do is sit there and drink my coffee. Oh yes. It will show up.

The man who would become my husband, and who is now my ex, was simultaneously attracted to me and repulsed. He begged for my hand in marriage two weeks after we met and didn't stop begging until I said yes. At the same time, he really didn't like me, but I didn't find that out until later.

He was confused. His and others' overwhelming response to me has caused no end of trouble as I try to guess what in the hell it is they want. I am only now understanding all this and taking steps to manage expectations.

But the best thing for me is to avoid people. I need to put my energy into where my Heavenly Father wants me to be. Empaths are well known for giving away their energy.

Empaths are also well known for having their energy taken against their will. Those energy suckers are *succubus* and *incubus*, female and male demons who only want to take, and never give anything but grief.

I've been on dance floors, having a great time with lots of upbeat people. Music giving to me. Endorphin release high. Then along comes an incubus. A man so needful he moves next to me and says, "There's something about you I need."

As if a spigot is turned on, I can physically feel my energy being sucked out and going straight into the man. He energizes and becomes happy as I tire and get sad. He does not understand why I will not dance with him again.

And what am I going to say to him? "You're an energy-sucking demon?" That definitely won't lessen my drama level, now will it? Besides, he doesn't know it.

The dead also like to hang around empaths. Three times I've experienced entire rooms of dead people. Of course, not literally dead, but dead in spirit.

The first time I was later than usual showing up to one of my favorite dance venues. I opened the front door to the restaurant area (the dance club was in the back) and remarked to myself that something was wrong.

I continued toward the loud music, fully expecting to see a floor full of bouncing people. Walking into the club, I saw four couples barely moving to a high-energy song. I looked around the room. Everybody else was *suspenditur animationem*.

I felt as if I were in a crypt. It was cold. The air was still.

One man turned his head to me. He smiled, and said loudly, "Angela's here!"

All heads turned to me. The DJ stood up straight. The dead smiled. Color went from gray to full-spectrum. I was asked to dance. I forced myself to stay, but after an hour I could no longer take the drain on my soul.

"Why are you leaving?" came the plaintive cries chasing me out the front door.

The second time was at a different dance venue I regularly habituated. Again, I was later than usual. (Usually I'm just about the first one there.) The band was kicking ass and taking names, but they were confused. Nobody was dancing. Nobody was moving.

I had walked in to another *suspenditur animationem*.

"Why aren't you people dancing?" I hollered. Yes, I hollered because the music was so loud. Everybody turned to me and one man wailed, "We don't know." Everybody else nodded agreement. They were confused. Well, to hell with that. So I said, "Get the hell off your butts and get up here."

I threw my purse and coat into a heap next to the bar in a corner, and ran out to the dance floor. The band smiled. One said, "Oh, thank God you're here." All of a sudden the floor was full, and the party was started. All they needed was for their key to be turned. I was the crank.

The third time I went into a Starbucks coffee shop. Handsome men, gorgeous women, delicious scents of coffee, beeping computers, loud grinders, hissing steam. All the makings of life, but I felt as if I were six feet under and the worms were coming for me.

An involuntary scream of horror came out of my mouth. Nobody noticed.

I ran out the door and to my car in a parking garage where I locked myself in and cried and wondered if I was doomed, never to be a part of human-kind, or to be loved, to be wanted, to have something given to me for no reason other than somebody loved me and not for what I could do for them.

I believe I am doomed in this matter. Of course, now the question is: Can I live with that state of being?

Most days the answer is yes. On those days I am content to be where I am. I can sit in my office — at my home — and go places in my mind one cannot buy a ticket to. I can be anybody, anywhere, at any age, in any time, and tell their stories.

I know this is so because when strangers hear my songs and read my words they always say, "How did you know that about *me?*"

It's because I listen to the stories nobody knows they are telling. Then I write about them.

first time for everything

first time for everything

A daily downpour carved out canyons in her soul.
She left him with the kids and drove away.
She ended in a little town she didn't know.
Contemplate the rest of her days.
Come the morning, she climbed upon the rocks.
He offered a steady hand.
Guess it's always true what they say:

There's a first time for everything.
There's a first time for everything.
There's a first time for everything.

There's a first time for everything.
There's a first time for everything.
There's a first time for everything.

Time was running fast, just like a tide.
In the lamplight, walk side by side.
Her mind replays that last night, again, again.
She tastes his tears, on her lips.
Come the morning, light creeps across their bed.
He stroked her hair, their souls were fed.
Guess it's always true what they say:

Oh! Oh! You should've seen his face.
Oh! Oh! And the way he called her name.
Yes.

There's a first time for everything.

Moments with him, every second, every word,
keep her strong and then she feels
his hands.

There's a first time for everything.
There's a first time for everything.
There's a first time for everything.

Chords

Am   G   F   Asus4   Asus2
Gsus4   Gsus 2   Fsus4   Fsus 2
Recommend judicious use of retard.
Don't be afraid to allow quiet moments to hang.
4/4 time. 120 tempo.

don't let this smile fool ya

It's hard to think when I've got a
man on my mind, so
don't let this smile fool ya.
I'm tight as a drum with
memories of love, aaah, ahh.
Don't let this smile fool ya.
They say what you see is
what you get, but
don't let this smile fool ya.

You see this smile?
Bright as the sun.
Listen to me good.
My heart's on the run.
Yeah, don't, don't, don't,
no-no please no.
Don't let this smile fool ya.

He called me baby, sugar pie, honey pot.
He said "Hot mama, show me whatcha got."

The night was hot. His eyes too blue.
I thought it meant I love you.
He was a dream I don't regret.
He was gone with the morning dew.

Have I seen better days? Too late for goodbye.
Don't let this smile fool ya.
Faceless nights. Nameless fears. Oh, oh, oh.
Don't let this smile fool ya.
Love burns bright, then comes the tears, so
don't let this smile —
The night was hot. Mmmmm.
The night was hot. Mmmmm.
Don't let this smile —
His eyes too blue. Oh, oh.
His eyes too blue. Oh, oh.
Don't let his smile fool ya.

Chords

F   G#   Bb   Cm   Fm   Ab
Sing with a smile, and a twinkle in your eye.
Fun bluesy.
4/4 time. 130-140 tempo.

time to time

verse:

Every now and then I get to thinking
you and I can make it, but then you
go and do something stupid, oh, oh, oh.
Every now and then I get to thinking we're
gonna be strong forever and then I stop wishing.

chorus:

Time to time my heart is broken by you.
Time to time I say I can't do this anymore.

verse:

Every now and then I get to thinking
you and I can start again, but
you can't leave well enough alone.
Every now and then I get to thinking
maybe this time is different, and I stop believing.

chorus:

Time to time my heart is broken by you.
Time to time I say I can't do this any more.

bridge:

Up and down. Spin around.
Hold me close, shut me down.
Tease me 'til I'm tight.
Where'd you go? Where are you?
Acting like you ain't got a clue.
Freeze. Me. Out. Of. Sight.

verse:

Every now and then I see you and
I think our course will change, but
we're still heading south.
Every now and then, very late at night
I remember your love, but then I
hang up the phone.
Oh.

chorus:

Time to time my heart is broken by you.
Time to time I say I can't do this anymore.

Chords

C Dm F G Am G Bb A
Sung clearly, definitively,
but with emotion.
4/4 time. 100 tempo.

twisting in the wind (I hate you)

"You only live once, so keep having fun"
are the words you said to me.
You may be right, and yes I do.
Still, your words, they haunt me.
You say I'm funny, and I make you laugh,
and we'll talk more later on.
But later never comes and I'm left
twisting in the wind.
Fun isn't all it's cracked up to be.
Substance must become sweet reality.
Yeah. Yeah. Oh, I hate you. Oh, I hate you.
For me you have a hunger.
When you sweet talk your voice is soft and low.
You make me believe I'm desperately wanted,
and from your words my desire grows,
but later never comes and I'm left
twisting in the wind. Oh, I hate you.
You're not here. Now comes my fun.
I pour it all out on other men.
They get my loving. It breaks my heart.
I can't wait for them to leave.
Oh, Oh, Oh, Twisting. Oh, Oh, Oh, Twisting.
I hate you.
You're jealous of temporary lovers
lighting up my nights.
You're happy they're gone,
your heart still wants me so, or so you say.
Here I go again, pouring myself into you,
the one man I want but can't seem to have.
But later never comes and I'm left
twisting in the wind. Yeah. Yeah. Oh.

Love is a seed, so the song goes.
And in the spring it becomes a rose.
Fun only cuts the heart open wide.
Soon it will be a large scar.
I don't only want to be just a fond memory of
what a man could handle in his prime.
Oh, I hate you. Why did you ask me to dance?
I hate you. Why did I take a chance?
I hate you. Why did you make love so fine?
I hate you? Why did I have to mind?
Can't get you out of my mind,
no matter how many times I'm left
twisting in the wind.
Fun isn't all it's cracked up to be.
Substance must become sweet reality.
Yeah. Yeah. Yeah, yeah.
Twisting. Twisting. Twisting.
Twisting in the wind.
Oh, I hate you.

Chords

Cm with rotating single notes
underneath of C   Bb   Ab   G
Recommend minimal use of retard.
3/4 time. Steady tempo at pace best for you.

girl living in color

She wishes rain to fall.
She wishes wind to blow.
She wishes chance to call.
She wishes you to know —

She's a girl living in color.
She's a girl living in color.

She's a girl living in color
in a black and white world.

In a black and white world.
In a black and white world.

She wishes hearts to fall.
She wishes kisses to   blow.
She wishes love to call.
She wishes you to know

She's a girl living in color.
She's a girl living in color.

She's a girl living in color
in a black and white world.

In a black and white world.
In a black and white world.

Chords

Bm over G. Am over G.
G   D   C   Em
Quiet, slow, lots of room.
90 tempo.

she's the leaving kind

She's the kind of woman you take to bed once.
Any more, and it will kill you.
She's the kind of woman that
makes you bump up against
oh, your limitations.
Yeah, yeah, she's the leaving kind.
Yeah, yeah, she's the leaving kind.

She's the kind of woman you never will forget no
matter who's laying beside you.
She's the kind of woman that brings a fond smile
but you tell another "I love you."

Yeah, yeah, she's the leaving kind.
Yeah, yeah, she's the leaving kind.

She's the kind of woman believes in true love,
wishes for it with all her might.
She's the kind of woman falls asleep in love's arms,
but wakes up alone in the night.

Yeah, yeah, she's the leaving kind.
Yeah, yeah, she's the leaving kind.

She's the kind of woman lays it all on the line,
even though she knows it will kill her.
She's the kind of woman
smiles through the pain as her
friends' husbands want her.

Yeah, yeah, she's the leaving kind.
Yeah, yeah, she's the leaving kind.

She's the kind of woman that will
turn a man's head.
Give him delusions of grandeur.
She's the kind of woman looks
forward to the day when
she will have a man of her own.

Yeah, yeah, she's the leaving kind.
Yeah, yeah, she's the leaving kind.

Chords

C   F   G (1-4-5 12-bar blues pattern)
Best with banjo and Bluegrass feel.
Stomp a foot in time on the 2 and the 4.
130+ tempo.

where the stallions run

Her eyes never leave Daddy's face
She hears Mama hit the floor.
Daddy hauls off, slaps Mama, and
she waits for his encore.
"Lay still, Mama, don't move."
This she says in her mind
as she peeks around the door,
the door she hides behind.

But Mama begs and pleads, and
she sees Daddy kick Mama's head.
She screams, "Stop it, Daddy, you'll kill
my mama dead."

Then she flies where the eagle soars.
Dives where the dolphin swims free.
She rides, she rides, she rides
where the stallions run.
Across the prairie
"You can't catch me."
And she rides.

Her eyes never leave Daddy's face
from where she lays thrown to the floor.
"Here's what you get for your troubles, girl."
She braces for more.
Mama watches from the corner, happy
it ain't her at his feet.
Mama does nothing to save the girl,
accepting her defeat.

Girl smiles up at Daddy
from her place on the floor.
She is free in her prison.
Pain she can ignore because she
soars with the eagle in bright places high.
Dives with the dolphin in the deep mystify.
Rides hard and fast where the stallions run.
Where the stallions run.
The girl doesn't plead. She refuses to beg.
She doesn't scream, "Stop it, Daddy,
or you'll kill me dead."
Because she
lies where the eagle soars.
Dives where the dolphin swims free.
She rides, she rides, she rides
where the stallions run.
Across the prairie.
"You can't catch me."
"You can't catch me."
"You can't catch me."
And she rides.

Chords

Bm   F#m   A   G
Ballad. Dark. Don't sing bright.
100 tempo.

sometimes love comes

Sometimes love comes early.

Sometimes love comes late.

Sometimes love doesn't come at all.

Heart and soul.

You wonder when you'll be whole.

Sometimes you feel warm and fuzzy.

Sometimes you ponder your fate.

Sometimes you only want to be called.

Heart and soul.

You wonder when you'll be whole.

Chords

C   Am   F   G
Blues Scale as intro, between verses,
and as outro:
C Bb G Gb F Eb C Bb C
Rubato. Emotional. Slow.
4/4 time. 80 tempo.

love can be so cold

She looked all of seventeen.
It was clear her heart was broke.
Maybe because I was a stranger.
Maybe because I was so old.
In any case, she turned to me and said,
"Love can be so cold.
Oh, love can be so cold."

                                "Why do you say this?
Is this all there is?"

Seems she loved a boy.
He promised her the moon. I said,
"Your natural first mistake was
believing him so soon."
In any case, I agreed with her.
Love can be so cold.
Oh, love can be so cold.

I said,
"In a hundred years your pain and heartbreak
won't matter one little bit."
In any case, I sighed,
"Love can be so cold.
Oh, love can be so cold."

She felt like a fool and was
running from her shame. I said,
"It's all new to you, girl,
but there's really no one to blame.
In every case," I said to her,
"Love can be so cold.
Oh, love can be so cold."

"How did you get so wise?"
I laughed but held back tears.

I said,
"I speak from experience of
many a long, long year.
Better to learn it now, that
Love can be so cold.
Oh, love can be so cold."

Love, love, love, love
Love, love, love, love
Love can be so cold.

Chords

Bm A Em
Use of instrumental stops recommended.
Sung cynically, hard-hearted.
100 tempo.

wednesday's child

She didn't know what day it was.
Last time she checked, it was Sunday.
She remembers because she walked out on the preacher.
Back when she knew each day as it completely happened,
her life was tightly ordered and oh so simple.

But she is Wednesday's Child
She is Wednesday's Child
and there is no denying.
No denying.

Lately she finds herself walking in the rain and storm.
Doesn't know where she's going so she kicks a stone.
Her sister was born late on Monday,
maybe early on Tuesday, in any case,
Sis was the pretty one and oh so graceful.

But she is Wednesday's Child
She is Wednesday's Child
and there is no denying.
No denying.

She's never confirmed suspicions, but
She must have been Wednesday born.
She's always walked under a cloud of woe.
If Thursday had been her day or
maybe even the last day of the week,
hard work might have paid off and she'd go far.

But she is Wednesday's Child
She is Wednesday's Child
and there is no denying.
No denying.

Friday and Sunday would have been better.
Loving, giving and smiling might be her days.

But she is Wednesday's Child
She is Wednesday's Child
and there is no denying.
No denying.

She didn't know what day it was.
Last time she checked, it was Sunday.
She remembers because she
walked out on
the preacher.

Chords

Eb   Gm   Dm   Cm
Sung without a lot of vocal range.
Quiet. Minimal instrumentation.
100 tempo.

wishes and snow

Twinkle again,
my little star.
I've never wandered
where you are.

Twinkle again.
Let it show.
I'll make wishes
when it snows.

I'll say again.
You were my star.
Where have you wandered?
You are so far.

I'll say again.
I want you to know.
My wishes melted
into the snow.

Hanging again
upon my star.
Looking for moonbeams
in a jar.

Hanging again.
I'm waiting slow
for wishes to rise
from the snow.

If wishes were
horses,
beggars would ride,
and I wouldn't feel
emptiness by my side.

If wishes were
horses,
I would flow
into your arms,
gentle like snow.

Wishes
and
snow.

Chords

Em C G Am
Recommend judicious use of retard.
Don't rush. Allow the lyrics to breath.
3/4 time. 100 tempo.

(sweet) affiliation

Affiliation
Restoration
Consolation
Imagination

I thought our affiliation *would*
bring about a restoration *but*
it was small consolation, *so I*
ended our affiliation, *and I*
sought other restoration, *but*
they were small consolation, *so I*
stopped my imagination.

Affiliation
Restoration
Consolation
Imagination

Our time is gone
Time, time marches on
Our love is gone.
My heart, heart marches on.

Affiliation
Restoration
Consolation
Imagination

I gathered my imagination, *and*
identified another consolation, *then*
prayed for my restoration *in this*
brand new affiliation, *but he*
didn't fire my imagination *like you*
did with your consolations *that*
every day gave me restoration *in our*
complicated affiliation.

Affiliation
Restoration
Consolation
Imagination

Our best time has begun.
Our time, time marches on.
Our best love has begun.

Our heart, heart marches on.
I'll give my best imagination *to*
bring about pure consolation *and I*
promise all for this restoration *in our*
sweet affiliation.

Chords

G   Am   D   C
Driving, steady beat.
4/4 timing. 120 tempo.

chanced upon a man

VERSE ONE: I

Gm	chanced upon a
Fm	man. He was
Gm	crying as he
Fm	walked. I
Gm	asked him
Fm	how he was.
Gm	He couldn't
Fm	talk. Yes, I
Gm	chanced upon a
Fm	man
Gm	cry-
Bb	-ing as he
Gm	walked.
Fm	*Music*
Gm	*Music*
Fm	*Music*

VERSE TWO: I

Gm	nodded my
Fm	head, and
Gm	made to
Fm	leave. He
Gm	put a hand
Fm	on my arm,
Gm	tugged at my
Fm	sleeve. Yes, he
Gm	put a hand on my
Fm	arm
Gm	tu------
Bb	---ugged at my
Gm	sleeve.
Fm	*Music*
Gm	*Music*
Fm	*Music*

VERSE THREE: He

Gm	stared at his
Fm	shoes, then
Gm	looked at the
Fm	sky. I
Gm	gave him a
Fm	hanky.
Gm	He wiped his
Fm	eyes. Yes, I
Gm	gave him a
Fm	hankeeeeeee-
Gm	-ee...He
Bb	wiped his
Gm	eyes.
Fm	*Music*
Gm	*Music*
Fm	*Music*

VERSE FOUR: He

Gm	stood straight and
Fm	tall. He
Gm	gave a sad
Fm	sigh. He said, "When
Gm	"loves comes you should
Fm	grab it.
Gm	Fear you should
Fm	defy. Yes, when
Gm	love comes
Fm	grab it.
Gm	Fear
Bb	you should
Gm	defy."
Fm	*Music*
Gm	*Music*
Fm	*Music*

OUTRO VERSE: I

Gm	chanced upon a
Fm	man.
Gm	He was
Fm	crying as he
Fm	walked. I
Gm	asked him
Fm	how he was.
Gm	He couldn't
Fm	talk. Yes, I
Gm	chanced upon a
Fm	man
Gm	[hold man]
Fm	[hold man]
Gm	cry-
Bb	-ing.
Gm	Chanced
Fm	upon a
Gm	man
Fm	MUSIC
Gm	Cryyyyyy
Fm	yyyyyyy
Gm	yyyyyyy-
Bb	-ing.
Gm	Chanced
Fm	Chanced
Bb	Chanced upon a
Gm	man.
Fm	*Music*
Gm	*Music*

Your backstory

your story

...can only be written by you. Each part of it is unique to you in its timing, yet these elements are not unknown to the human race. In fact, they are what define us as humans. They are experiences we share with others in story, poetry, and song.

Some say poetry and song are the same. I can understand their point of view, though I believe equating them deprives each of their singular power. Poetry and song are not the same. They may trade places occasionally. But when vocal tonal variations, along with pitch, pace, power, and mechanical instrumentation are added to poetry, then it ceases to be poetry.

It is a song. The listener knows this, and reacts accordingly.

It has been suggested that the brain reacts faster and better and more broadly to voice than to music. In this I would agree. Sales of instrumental works are not nearly as high as works with vocals accompanied by instrumentation.

There are exceptions, but they are the ones that prove the rule.

'Tis the same with our lives.

In the following pages, I invite you to use *your* words, *your* pitch, pace, and power, and tell *your* story. I know the modern way of writing poetry often excludes old-fashioned rhyme patterns.

Don't eschew the use of rhyme.

Rhyme is a powerful tool that allows your brain to explore new ways of expression that often clarifies thought. ***Use it.***

How did you get here?

Where are you going?

What challenges do you have?

What good has happened?

What good *is* happening?

What do you do now?

Turn the page and begin.

attach a large picture of yourself here
that reflects the inner you,
or the *you* you want to become.

your story

your story

your story

_____

_____

_____

_____

_____

_____

_____

_____

_____

_____

_____

your story

your story

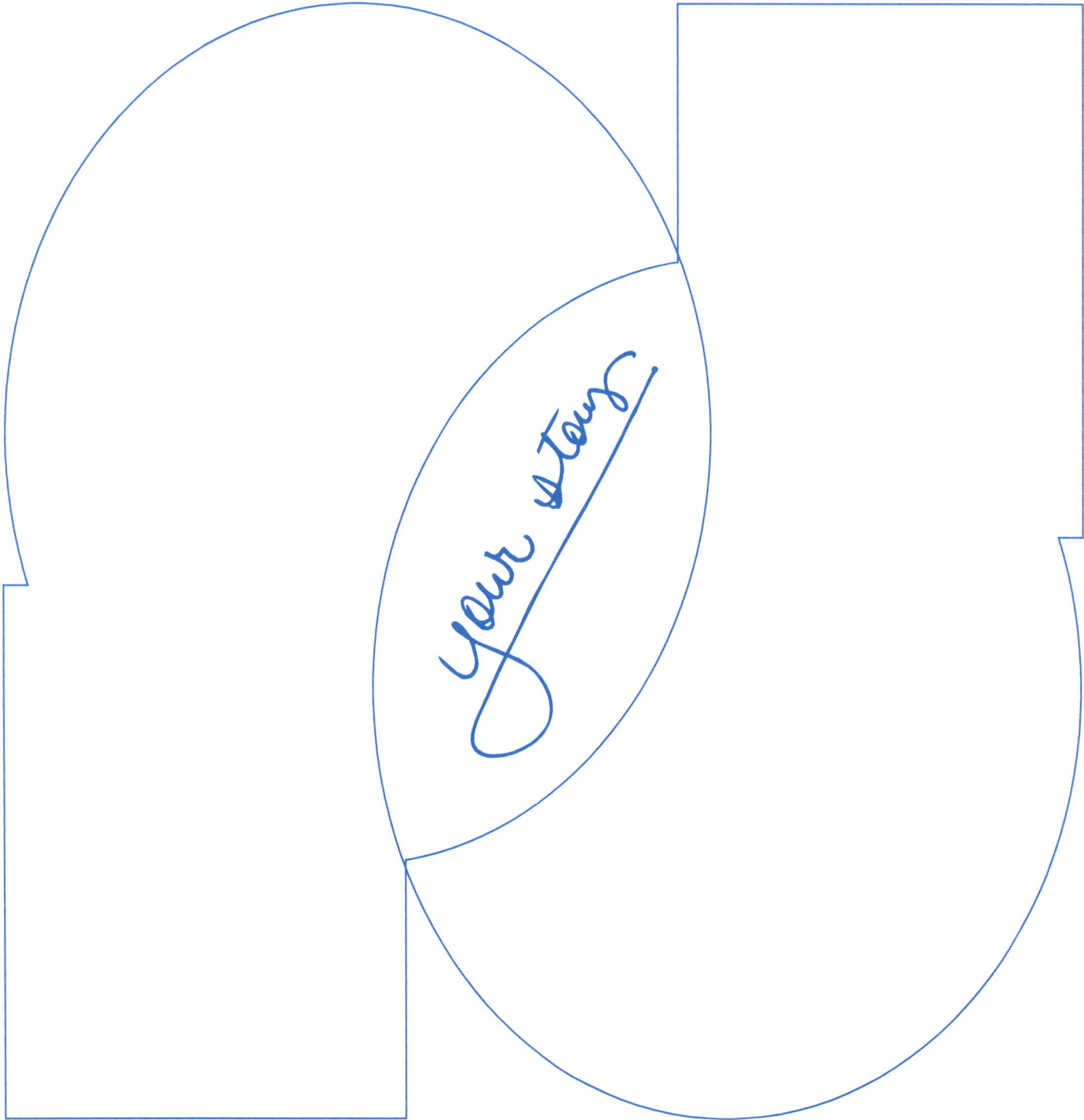

Your story

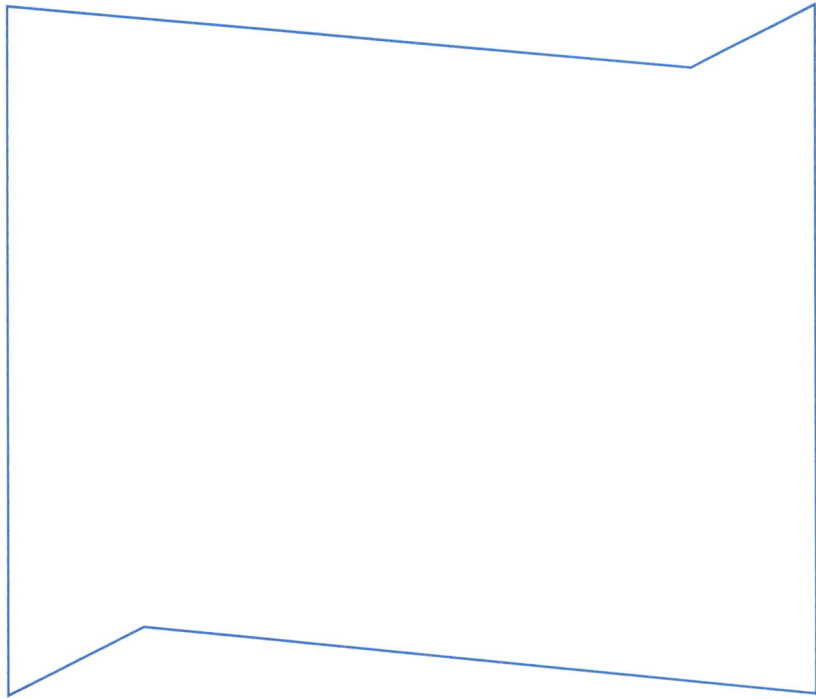

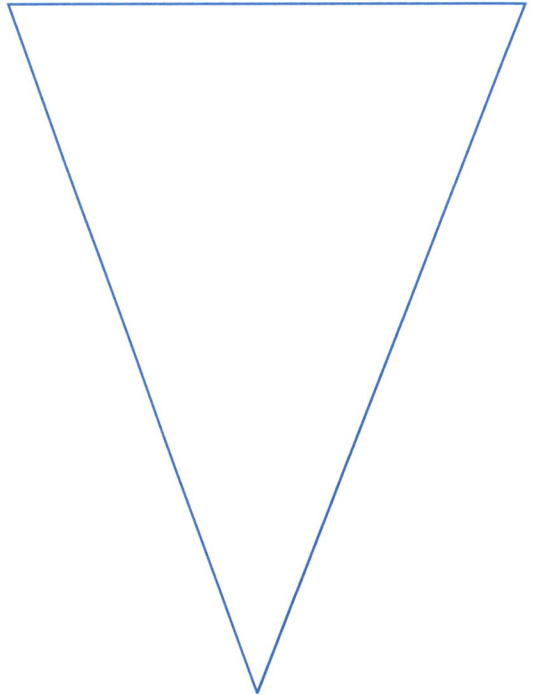

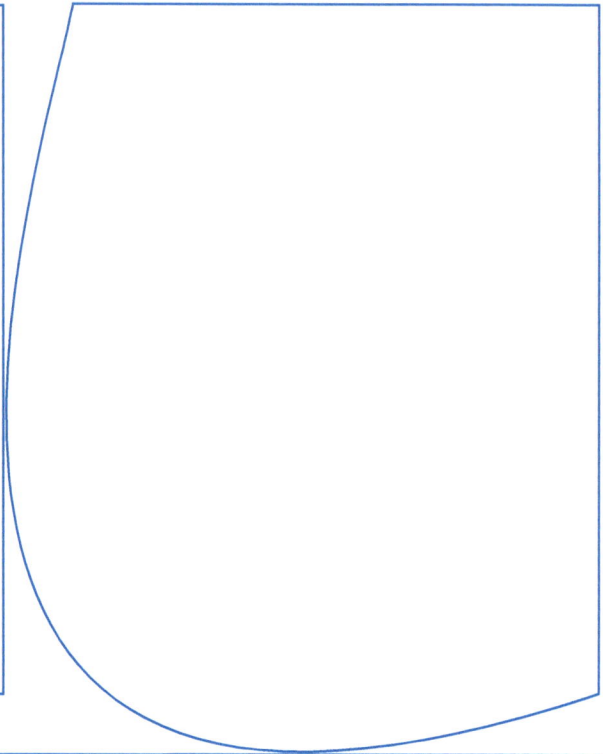

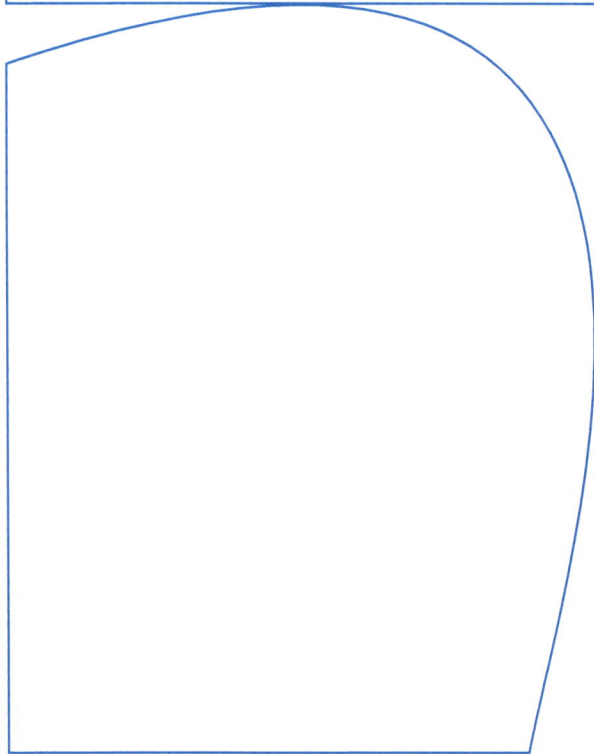

first time for everything

BUSINESS BOOKS
by ANGELA K. DURDEN:
Nine Stupid Things People do to Mess Up
Their Resumés (2000)

MEN! K.I.S.S. Your Resumé and Say Hello
to a Better Job (2013)
Also available as audio from Audible

LADIES! K.I.S.S. Your Resumé and Say
Hello to a Better Job (2013)

Opportunity Meets Motivation (2010)

Navigating the New Music Business as a
DIY and Indie: Coming Clean with the
Down and Dirty (2015)

CHILDREN'S BOOKS by AKD:
A Mike and His Grandpa Series:
Heroes Need Practice, Too! (2006)
The Balloon That Would Not Pop! (2012)

OTHER BOOKS by AKD:
Eloise Forgets How to Laugh (2010)
Twinkle, a memoir (2015)

FICTION by DURDEN KELL:
Whitfield, Nebraska (2015)

TWO NOVEL SERIES
IN DEVELOPMENT:
The Case Files of Smith and Jones:
The Case of the Cotton Fiber Snuff Tape
The Case of the Cat-Loving Killer
The Case of the Angelic Assassin

The Dance Floor Wars:
Dispatches from the Front
Lucinda's People
Life Cycle of a Fling
Collisions

978-0-9854623-1-4
First Time for Everything
Publisher: Writer for Hire!
Imprint: Second Bight

9 780985 462314 >